Truth and Life
~ Made Simple ~

"Your" Simple Answers To Life's Tough Questions

Inspired at the Holy Family
Adoration Chapel, Orlando, FL

MICHAEL CARR

TRUTH AND LIFE MADE SIMPLE
"YOUR" SIMPLE ANSWERS TO LIFE'S TOUGH QUESTIONS
INSPIRED AT THE HOLY FAMILY ADORATION CHAPEL,
ORLANDO, FL

iUniverse books may be ordered through booksellers or by contacting:

iUniverse
1663 Liberty Drive
Bloomington, IN 47403
www.iuniverse.com
1-800-Authors (1-800-288-4677)

Because of the dynamic nature of the Internet, any web addresses or links contained in this book may have changed since publication and may no longer be valid. The views expressed in this work are solely those of the author and do not necessarily reflect the views of the publisher, and the publisher hereby disclaims any responsibility for them.

Any people depicted in stock imagery provided by Thinkstock are models, and such images are being used for illustrative purposes only.
Certain stock imagery © Thinkstock.

ISBN: 978-1-4917-6462-6 (sc)
ISBN: 978-1-4917-6463-3 (e)

Library of Congress Control Number: 2015905089

Print information available on the last page.

iUniverse rev. date: 05/08/2015

Table of Contents

Table of Contents

Table of Contents

Table of Contents

10 REASONS WHY

* You must begin reading this book with the section titled "How This Book Was Born".

1. **"Your" Initial journey** through this book will be guided from here
2. **"Your" Learning and inspiration** will ignite you to help others see the way
3. **"Your" Answers you're seeking,** will be less mysterious and easily understood
4. **'Your" Desire to get "Your" life right** will happen quickly
5. **"Your" Understanding** of simple things, which you've made complex, will be apparent
6. **"Your" Ability to be liked** (especially by "your" loved ones) will amaze you
7. **'Your" Awareness** of how to reduce "your" selfishness will be immense and easy
8. **"Your" Courage to admit** you're not perfect and you make mistakes will be freeing
9. **"Your" Old ways will be replaced** with a fresh start attitude and thinking
10. **"Your" Life Depends on it** – and 'Your" marriage, family, friendships, career etc.

A special and sincere thanks to:

Teresa (a.k.a. "Classyteach") –
Thank you for your superior command of the English language, your honest friendship and for;
"Breathing literary Truth, Life and Simplicity" into this book.

Majela (Manager, The Cadillac Hotel, Miami, FL) –
Thank you for your graciousness and the inspiring oceanfront room. This enabled me to the complete the final components of this book at the "Cadillac".
"The Truth in Life is Simply what you did for me, YOU cared".

Father William Ennis (Pastor, Holy Family Catholic Church, Orlando, FL) –
Thank you for taking the manuscript and reading it on your trip to Ireland. When you offered to help launch this book at Holy Family, it was another confirmation that this book has a <u>"Guided Destiny"</u>.
"You are making the Truth and Life of this book Simply "AWESOME"

The Good Lord above – You get all the gracious thanks and praise –
"You have allowed me to understand that, Truth in Life through you, can be Simple, if I'll just ASK"

Acknowledgements

There are some very special people that without them this book could not have been possible. These friends and family members that have encouraged and inspired me to bring this book to life are among my most cherished.

It is through their contributions and constant encouragement that has allowed me to realize, this book is bigger than anything I could have dreamed of.

First, and foremost I must thank the good Lord above for selecting me to be an instrument of His work. This may sound like an exaggeration to some, but know this, I am not a writer but the Lord chose me for some reason to bring forth these messages He wants people to read.

Mandy Digiammarino - To my most treasured and trusted friend. I thank you for all you have done. You have provided me with a clear vision and purpose for the material in this book. I thank you for your excellent photography skills (LOL), in taking the pictures of the hand written versions of these poems. I want to express my sincere appreciation for your skill in deciphering my hand writing. I could not have done it without you. You and Luke are my family and I love you very much.

Taylor Carr, my Daughter (My Boo) – You have helped me realize how precious life is and how short life can be. You've also showed me how important it is to make the adjustments now and not to wait. You bring such great joy to my Life. Thanks for giving your Dad a break, I love you kid!

Acknowledgements

Jackson Carr, my Son (Jax) – You have brought me to realize how important it is to love, forgive and to listen before I speak. I think I learn more from you, than you do from me. You bring such happiness to my life and you inspire me more than you know. I love you man! Keep hoopin'.

Kim Hanley – My neighbor, friend and constant encourager. Thank you for painstakingly interpreting the handwritten versions of these poems. Without your relentless encouragement and typing skills; in addition to your friendship and understanding, I may still be typing these poems myself. You, Kyle, Charlie and Alex are special to me.

Nancy Harnish – The "Keeper of the Prayer Books" (Where I had written these poems at the Holy Family Adoration Chapel). If we hadn't bumped into each other that day in the chapel, I may not have found the poems I had written. Consequently, this book may have never become a reality. I am certain it was the work of the Holy Spirit. There are no coincidences. It was just time for these poems to be published. I appreciate you very much!

Aunt Mary Krafchak and Aunt Dawn Browne – (a.k.a. my surrogate Moms) - With the two of you providing me your wisdom, inspiration, patience and love, this became fuel for me to understand my direction and purpose with this book. I thank you, I admire you and most of all I love you!

Polly – If it had not been for you having the courage, to do what was needed to be done, this book may have never been written. I am truly sorry. I hope one day you'll find it in your heart to forgive me.

How This Book Was Born

I want to provide you the story of how this book was born. I will share with you many things, some not so pleasant. I will also keep in mind, for your sake, it is not all the sordid details that are important.

I believe it is more important to share with you the lessons, behaviors and implications of our actions or inaction that can be the true destroyer of marriages, families and relationships.

I vividly remember January 10th 2006 at 9:10 am. I am standing next to the stairway leading upstairs to my children's bedrooms, and that instant, my life changed forever. My wife walked up to me and said, "I want a divorce." Like most men, I couldn't understand why. I had tried to understand right there on the spot why she wanted to divorce me. Again, like most men it wasn't as apparent to me as it was to her.

There had been times previously that she had said this and I had tried to change her mind. However, this time her mind was completely made up. She had endured enough. We were married for eighteen years and together for twenty-three. We were blessed with two amazing children, Taylor our daughter and Jackson our son. At the time Taylor was twelve years old and Jackson was nine. Polly my wife, was the only woman whom I had ever loved and now our marriage was about to be over and our family broken up.

I knew there were things I needed to improve upon and I didn't take them as seriously as I should have. I thought we would be together for life and that there was plenty of time to work on these things. Well, as I now know, time is of the essence, especially with the people we love the most.

How This Book Was Born

I do not fault Polly, for making the decision she did. I truly wish I had been smarter and more attentive to her needs. As the story would go, I had visited the Adoration Chapel at Holy Family Church a myriad of times prior to this divorce announcement. In 2005, however, I began going to the Adoration Chapel more frequently. It's a small, quaint place that accommodates about forty people. If there were forty people there, it would be packed to the gills. Usually there are only a small number of people there at any given time, but there is always someone in the Chapel.

I found great peace at the Adoration Chapel. I began to understand things and to see that I needed to make some changes. I was introduced to some guys that were "Emmaus Brothers". Not knowing what an Emmaus Brother was, I asked. The next thing I knew, I was being encouraged to attend a three day Emmaus Retreat. My Emmaus sponsors were Bud Bennington, Michael Hanley and Ralph Rodriguez-Torres. These guys had no idea how influential they would be in my life.

I went to the retreat. I found it enlightening. Unfortunately, I wasn't hit with any lightning bolts of awakening. I guess I wasn't quite ready yet. I can be a bit remedial at times, (it's alright to laugh at that).

Upon my return from the Emmaus Retreat, I began going to the Adoration Chapel more frequently. Its open twenty-four hours a day, and I found myself taking advantage of many of those hours. As I would sit quietly, I would say some prayers and ask God to make me a better man, a smarter man and ask to be enlightened. I asked for all the usual stuff we ask for when things are not going our way. I did not seem to be hearing any of the answers I was looking for. So some days, I would leave the chapel more confused and frustrated than when I went in. I continued to go to the chapel, nonetheless.

How This Book Was Born

I was there one day and noticed a small journal-type book on the credenza in the atrium, which is just outside the chapel. I picked it up and noticed that people had written prayer requests in it, so I figured it couldn't hurt. As I was thinking what I should write, a thought came to me. It was as if someone was whispering it to me, but I was the only one standing there. So I wrote what I thought I was hearing in the prayer book. It was short and to the point, nothing poetic or earth shattering. Over the next several days, I would write these prayer requests in the prayer book, **now here's where it gets interesting.**

One day, I was in the chapel praying for God to straighten me up and steer me in the right direction. It was at that time I heard something inside me saying, "Many Days Go By", but it wasn't a passing thought. More words began to fill my head and the more I listened to these words, the more I knew I should write them down. I got up and went out to the atrium where the prayer book was on the credenza. I picked it up and began writing what I was hearing in my head.

There were a lot of words swirling around in my head and I was having a hard time keeping up with writing these words in the prayer book. In a matter of minutes, I read what I was writing and to my surprise it looked like a poem. Of course because I was writing so fast, I felt the need to go back and edit the work a bit to make it look like English.

As I read what I had written, or was actually "inspired to write", surprisingly I found that I had written a poem that actually made sense. I titled it "Many Days Go By". It's the first poem in this book (written 7/1/05). I believe it was the Holy Spirit telling me that many days are going by and I'm not doing what I'm supposed to be doing. I initially did not understand it and felt it was the message someone was trying to give me.

How This Book Was Born

It was about six months later from 7/1/05 (the date when the first poem was written), that my wife told me she wanted a divorce. I was being given the answer and the time to make the changes that were needed to save our marriage and our family. However, being in my current selfish mindset, I didn't get the warning. So therefore, we paid the price of the dissolution of our marriage and our family being broken apart.

That wasn't the only chance I was given, just the first one (That I saw, I'm sure there were plenty of other signs I missed). Even about a year prior to Polly telling me she wanted a divorce, I was in the chapel and I began listening a little more intently when I was there. The same type of thought or message came to me as clear as if someone was telling me. Now, there were no voices or apparitions. I'm not that special! But the thoughts were very clear. Here is what I heard:

> - "Honor, Polly, Taylor and Jackson"
> - "It is the beginning of your time"
> - "Your Christ-likeness will grant you all that you seek "

I was so confused, I even went home and told Polly what I had heard, and yes, I got one of "those" looks.

So I kept thinking about the three things I had heard and what they meant. Of course, being a guy, I took it as all my troubles were through. After all, I did hear, it was the beginning of "MY" time. Unfortunately, I wasn't listening with my adult grown up ears. I was listening with my, "life is all about me" ears. Guess what? I got the wrong message. As I say these words to myself now, they have much greater meaning. "My Christlikeness", means, I need to become selfless versus selfish. I need to mature and grow in my love for others. "It's the beginning of your time" means, it's time to realize I am responsible to and for others, not just myself. Then there is the "Honoring" part;

How This Book Was Born

this means I need to put my family first, in particular and especially, my wife Polly, my daughter Taylor and my son Jackson.

I really wish I could have received that message ten or so years ago. I love my Family so much and wish our marriage could have been restored. That would be awesome. It would truly take an Act of God for that to happen, but my time has passed me for that. I still have my two wonderful kids, Taylor is now twenty-two yrs old and Jackson is eighteen. Polly has since remarried someone she met after she left, and has elected not to speak to me anymore. I know the hurt and pain I have caused her and if she chooses not to speak to me, that is her decision. I do wish however, for the sake of the kids, we could talk about them from time to time.

Here is a really neat thing that has happened. Now that much time has passed and I have learned so much about many different things. Now when I go to the Adoration Chapel at Holy Family, my mind is much more receptive to listening to the messages I hear. Since the first poem was written in July of 2005, there have been over 200 poems written. This book contains the initial 121 poems. These poems are the building blocks of new thinking, new learning and greater understanding of what it takes to begin to be the person, I have always wanted to become. It is the result of our divorce and the subsequent journey that has begun a new motivation and desire to become a better man, a better father, a better friend and one day a "Really Desirable Christ-like Husband".

The actual moment the book was born...

I went to the chapel one day and I saw someone I knew, Nancy Harnish. Now keep this in mind for my future statements below. Nancy and I were the only two people in the chapel that day (It is very rare when there are only two people in the chapel, there are usually

How This Book Was Born

others present). I had known Nancy for some time she used to teach my daughter Taylor in P.R.E.P. classes (religious studies). Nancy knew my wife Polly; and I had not seen Nancy for a long time. I said hello to her, and she inquired about my wife. Obviously she wasn't aware that Polly had left me about three years earlier. When I told her of this, she felt very bad. But I did not want her to feel so bad. That's when I let her know since Polly left, I had been coming to the chapel quite frequently. As a result of that, a really awesome thing has happened. I told Nancy that when I am in the chapel, I get inspired to write poems and that I think that I may have written about forty or so poems in the prayer books.

Now here is where it gets really interesting... I said to Nancy, "I would love to have those poems just to see what I had written, because, after I write them, I have no idea what I had written". I could not even tell you one line from any of the poems. THAT IS HOW I KNOW THEY ARE NOT MY WORDS, BUT WORDS THAT ARE INSPIRED.

When I told Nancy about this, she replied "I'm responsible for the prayer books, and I have all of them". Well, you can only imagine my surprise. This surely was not a coincidence! Nancy said I was welcome to take the prayer books and look through them". I was still stunned. I realized for the first time somebody wanted this book to be born and I think I now know who!

I then decided to collect up all the prayer books from the chapel. The reason for this is, you can't take the pages out of the prayer book, this kind of defeats a purpose of a prayer book. Nonetheless, I picked up thirty-five prayer books. each book was about 250 pages double sided. So if you do the math, this would be 17,500 pages that would need to be reviewed to find all the poems I had written. I then enlisted the help of my good friend Mandy DiGiammarino.

How This Book Was Born

She came to my house and we began going through the prayer books page by page.

After about 5 ½ hours of flipping 17,500 pages and taking pictures of all the poems I had written, we arrived at the total number of poems. I thought there would be about forty or so. To my amazement, it turns out I had written 121 poems! You can only imagine my reaction. Here I am thinking I had written 40 poems and turns out to be three times that many.

Now here is something else, that's very interesting… No two poems had the same title or content. There are some that were similar with recurring themes, but each had its own uniqueness. This was confirmation, it was not my work. I was just a guy, with a pen in my hand, who was being inspired to write. Hard to believe? for some this might be true, but not for me. Remember, I was there. I was the guy with the pen. Keep in mind, I am not a writer!

Here's is the truly defining time… and most likely the moment when I realized this was bigger than just writing poems in the chapel…

As I would go to the chapel some days, I would walk in and the prayer book would be open to a page to one of the poems I had written. I thought, Wow! This is really amazing. People were actually reading them!!

The "Ah Ha" moment…

I began seeing comments and compliments on the pages where the poems had been written. There were probably at least a couple dozen compliments on various poems that I saw. But this one compliment in particular was the key message to me that these poems were much bigger than me just writing them in prayer books in the chapel. This one particular compliment looked to be written by a woman with

How This Book Was Born

very elegant hand writing. The compliment was this, *"Michael your poems are beautiful, don't ever stop writing them, they help me in my life"*, and she signed it.

When I saw what this woman had written, that was confirmation that this book needs to be published and put in the hands of many people. Today, people still write compliments on the poems. The compliments consist of thanking me for the poems and how the messages and encouragement they receive helps them in their lives. This is a great blessing.

But again, it is important to remember, these words are inspired words and not mine. They are merely on loan for me to use and to share with you and as many people who need them.

That's how this book was born...

One final thought, when reading these poems it will be like looking at the cloud shapes in the sky. No two people may see or interpret them in the same way.

"YOU" are reading the poems, so the inspiration you'll receive will be tailored to YOU.

Again, No coincidence!

In Love,
~ Michael ~

Many Days Go By (Part 1 of 2)

Many days go by.
With lonely nights to follow,
Many days go by.
As her heart, is filled with sorrow.

Many days go by.
Without a glimmer of hope,
Many days go by.
Another day, I acted like a dope.

Many days go by.
As I admire her from a-far.
Many days go by.
I remember when I was her star.

Many days go by.
More opportunity slips away.
Many days go by.
I hope I've earned, the right to stay.

Many days go by.
I feel her love begin to wane.
Many days go by.
I remember again, I've caused her pain.

1

Many days go by.
I believe she's drifting away.
Many days go by.
Alone on the couch I lay.

Many days go by.
I wonder if ever I'll recover.
Many days go by.
I wonder if she'll find another.

Many days go by.
I try so hard, to no avail.
Many days go by.
Another expectation, I did fail.

Many days go by.
I pray and pray with all my heart.
Many days go by.
All my dreams seem shattered apart.

Many Days Go By (Part 2 of 2)

Many days go by.
I sit and think and worry and cry.
Many days go by.
I wonder, if I have the strength to try.

Many days go by.
I think and think, but take little action.
Many days go by.
With little reward or satisfaction,

Through these many days I pray,
That soon the blues will go away.

As I climb this flat-surfaced wall,
It always seems I slip and fall.

I know I must continue to fight.
To give up now just wouldn't be right.

I love them much,
I love them all.
Because of my family,
I will stop this fall.

To turn around but not look back,
I must hang tough and stay on track.

I build this prose to finish strong,
And to realize this fight has been long.

You Can't Change
The *TRUTH*
But, The *TRUTH,*
Can Change . . .
YOUR LIFE . . .
It's *SIMPLE*!

But know that I will succeed.
It's because, inside, I have this need.

For I love my family more than life itself,
To lie down now would be no help.

Please hear me now: no further can I go.
Lord, please send me help, but not too slow.

Yes, my son, I will… you know.

In Love,
~ *Michael* ~

10/13/05   **Keep My Faith Strong**

Keep my faith strong, steer me right.
I don't want to fail, give me strength to fight.

I love you, Lord. Please guide me, and show me your way.
I want to be healthy and smart, and not just okay.

An abundant prosperous life, is what I aspire,
But doing it my way, too fast I will tire.

My faith is strong, in your way I feel.
Be patient and forgiving with me, as before you I kneel.

I'm ready to get it right now, yes, it's about time.
In keeping my faith strong, I've been a bit sublime.

Keeping faith is one part of it, but you need to believe and expect.
Be bold, but respectful in asking, and the Lord will provide and protect.

So keep your faith alive, and growing stronger every day.
Your faith is a stepping stone, to understanding God's way.

In Love,
~Michael~

7/25/05   **My Trust Is With YOU**

My trust is with YOU,
Please make me new.

My hope comes from YOU,
Help see me through.

My love is directed by YOU,
I'm only one, but need the strength of two.

My understanding is inspired by YOU,
Show me what you'd have me do.

In Love,
~Michael~

7/30/05   **I Look To You**

I look to you for guidance, truth, wisdom,
Understanding and love.
These virtues have escaped me,
Please send them now from above.

I feel I miss signs sometimes,
Please make these things clear to me,
So that I may become the person,
You are trying to make me.

I try to keep my eyes open,
So the better I will see;
The times you are showing,
The person you need me to be.

I look to you to guide me,
To the things I need to do;
But I must be responsible
For watching out for you.

Looking and watching;
Is only part of it.
Get up and take some action,
And on my hands, no longer sit.

In Love,
~Michael~

8/20/05   **Be With Me**

Be with me,
Show me what to do.
Help me to be
A bit more like you.

Wherever I go,
I hope you'll find my way;
To watch over and follow me,
Both night and day.

When I know you're there,
And I'm within your sight;
I feel brave and confident,
And feel no fright.

Be with me,
My whole life long;
That when I'm weak,
You'll make me strong.

In Love,
~ Michael ~

8/29/05   **Guide Me This Day**

Guide me this day,
Show me your way.

Grant me the wisdom,
And understanding I desire.
Put back inside of me,
That great stirring fire.

Give me the strength I need,
To forge ahead and not to heed.

Guide me this day,
And please change my way,
For I no longer,
I'm sorry, do I want to say.

As you guide,
I feel you inside.
You are the strength I need,
To flow, with this rising tide.

In Love,
~ Michael ~

9/7/05   **I Feel You With Me**

I feel you with me,
When my heart is aware,
I'm not always listening;
So I don't always hear.

But know that I long,
To hear you every day;
I will continue to believe,
Everyday when I pray.

I love you, Lord Jesus,
I'm humbled by your love,
I know you are walking with me;
And guiding from above.

I look to you,
To open my heart.
It's hard to begin again;
Starting over from the start.

Because I feel you with me,
I will have no fear,
I know you're always with me;
I can feel you when you're near.

In Love,
~ Michael ~

11/18/05   I Trust In You

I trust in you,
With my heart and soul.

It is only you,
That can make me whole.

Your love your faith,
None can compare.

You've taken on pain,
For us, you spare.

I love you much Lord,
I give you my heart.

Do not let the enemy,
Keep us apart.

In Love
~Michael~

11/22/05   Thanks For Keeping Me Near

Thanks for keeping me near.
Thanks for letting me hear.

I know you're there watching me,
Giving me vision to see;

This wonderful place,
You've allowed me to be.

I ask you dear Lord,
Don't stop believing in me.

In Love
~Michael~

12/17/05 **I Pray To You Today**

I pray to you today,
To show you that I may;

Be able to love better than before,
And praise you a little more.

To say that, I'm ready to heal,
Is why I come before you, and kneel.

I've messed up things long enough,
My way, was too tough.

I pray to you today,
That you show me, a better way.

When you are in control,
Safe is my heart and my soul.

So I pray to you today,
That its time, I find my new way.

In Love
~Michael~

12/19/05   **I Come To You To Pray**

I come to you,
To pray,
To thank you for,
Each and every day.

Your love, your trust,
For me is a must.

They make me whole,
In my heart and soul.

Let me see the light,
And not give up the fight.

There are times I see,
That life, gets the best of me.

But I am strong,
And will persevere long.

I come to you to pray Lord,
In hopes that you will guide.
Light my path for me each day,
So the pains, of my heart, will subside.

In Love
~ Michael ~

12/20/05   **How I See Him…**
(Seeing Through Polly's Eyes)

I've written before, and I'll write more.
I have more love than ink, and you wonder and think.

Where does he get these words and rhymes,
It must be, the 20 plus years and times.

He has always written, he has always had love.
At this point in time, he turns to the Lord above.

I think he sees, the changes he's had.
He was unhappy, but now he's glad.

He owes me so much,
He loves my kiss, He loves my touch.

His hands are like magic, his kiss divine.
I love him, I love him, and he's all mine.

Where did he learn, to write these lines,
It must be experience, from his life and times.

He looks to the Lord, for his strength each day,
And promises me, the new him…is here to stay.

He swept me away, with his eyes and his smiles.
His journey has been filled, with many long and tough miles.

I tingle when he kisses me, I melt, when he hugs.
I look into his eyes, and it's he, who I love.

This poetry talent, I knew not he had,
But, when he writes about me, it makes me feel glad.

He tells me, the Lord has told him, great things are coming our way.
He's stopped living in past, and is living in the now today.

I love Him…

In Love,
~ Michael ~

12/20/05   I Come To You And Kneel

I come to you,
And kneel and pray,
To understand how to be,
Better tomorrow, than I was today.

I seek your help,
So I may grow,
In keeping my faith strong,
And my heart a glow.

At times I don't try,
As hard as I could,
You've given me gifts and said;
Use them, I should.

I need you Lord,
To show me how;
To use the gifts, you've given me,
Beginning here and now.

I come to you and kneel,
And say please be my guide;
There are things inside of me,
I no longer want to hide.

In Love
~Michael~

12/20/05 **My Son, My Gift**

My Jax, My Jax,
I'm so blessed to have you here,
The Lord has gifted me,
Just by having you near.

You're special, so special,
You're my gift, from above,
Know you are the greatest,
And my son, that I love.

To watch you run, to play, and to learn,
It's awesome to see,
You are so great,
I learn more from you... then you from me.

I thank you my son,
My blessed one.

I pray to God, for me to be, a great Dad –
I miss that... Because...
It's something, I never had...

You will be great,
The Lord has said,
Remember this...
Keep the Lord, in your heart, your hands, and your head.

Look to HIM, for help and love,
For it is HE, who watches over you, from above.

~ In Love, DaD ~
(To: My Son Jackson)

12/20/05   **Tay My Love**

Tay Tay, you're awesome,
I love you tomorrow, I Love you today,
I'm so proud of you,
You are special in every way.

It's my privilege, to be your Dad
I love being with you,
You're my special girl,
And most of all, my special "Boo".

You're smart, you're pretty,
You're the greatest kid,
Marrying your Mom, and having you,
Is one of the greatest things, I ever did.

You're the best, I you love much,
I love your kiss, I love your hug.

I know, you're my boo,
But you're Mom's, love bug too.

God bless you my love,
Remember... You are watched and protected
By Angels above.

~ In Love, DaD ~
(To: My Daughter Taylor)

6/8/06   **A Simple Poem**

A simple poem,
From me to you,
To let you know,
It's coming true;

What you said,
I did hear,
My prayers to you,
You held them near.

I thank you Lord,
For my eyes to see,
For my ears to hear,
And that you've set me free.

My love for your love,
Grows ever stronger,
My faith in you,
Lasts a lifetime longer.

So keep it simple,
Keep me on track,
Keep me moving forward,
My old ways, I don't want back.

In Love
~Michael~

7/1/06   **I Seek The Truth**

I seek the truth,
So I look within,
Not always finding it,
And obtaining the win.

But know that, I will not stop,
Until I reach the way;
When I'm quiet,
And hear you say;

"Fear not my son, for I am with you.
See life with Joy, not as one, but as two;
For it is within you,
To find, true Love in all you do".

"Make peace with the Past,
And forever your happiness will last".

"Keep seeking the truth,
And you will find,
That what's in front of you,
Is more important, than what's behind".

Note: Based on thinking of my wife who has left me.

In Love,
~ Michael ~

10/31/06   **The Hardest Thing**

Lord please help me,
I've hurt my one true love,
She's gone and not looking back,
Please protect her from above.

The things I've done,
Have caused hurt and distrust.
Being healed and made healthy,
By you, is a must.

My wife has left me,
And she had every right to,
I didn't treat her, in a Christlike way,
And now, I cry out to you.

I don't deserve her back,
And that's very clear to see,
But I ask you Dear Lord, let her find it in her heart,
To please, one day forgive me.

This is the hardest thing,
I ever had to do,
When she left, my heart went with her,
Please heal us both, all my faith is in you.

Please bring my family back together...

In Love,
~Michael~

11/28/06   **I Hurt Sometimes**

I hurt sometimes,
When I am sad.
I've done dumb things,
This makes me mad.

I wish, I wish,
The pain away,
But it takes a while,
For it, to go its way.

But there is one thing,
I do know,
It's through you, to heaven,
I'll eventually go.

I look to the sky and say,
Thank you Lord for all you do,
Now show me Lord, what it is,
That I can do for you.

I hurt sometimes,
When I live in the past.
Lift me up and beyond,
So my hurt, no longer lasts.

In Love
~Michael~

12/5/06   **Every Day I Pray**

Dear Lord,
Everyday I pray,
Asking you,
To show me, the way.

You answer me,
But I don't always hear,
Even though, I know,
You are very near.

I will do your will,
To the best I can be,
So that I will be with you,
For all eternity.

But for now, as I stumble through,
And try to put aside my ways,
I pray that you will guide me,
To more productive days.

In Love
~Michael~

1/1/07   **I will Trust**

I will trust in you.
My future you must guide.
I want to let the love out,
That's been bottled up inside.

I've been hurt by someone,
I used to trust and love.
I believe we were brought together,
By special Angles, from above.

I gave my heart and soul to her,
In hopes, that she would care,
But I found out, that was not to be,
The same feelings, she would share.

The time has passed for her to be,
A special part of my heart,
I must move forward without her,
And begin a fresh new start.

But I will trust, and love again,
In the time, that is supposed to be,
You can't rush love, so I'll take the time,
To make me, a better me.

In Love
~Michael~

2/19/07   **Show Me Lord**

Show me Lord,
And Let me learn,
Lift me up,
With great discern.

I vow to love,
To live, to laugh,
In hopes to meet,
The right, better half.

I laugh, I cry,
I don't know why.

I know you'll be,
Proud of me.

Show me Lord,
Sometimes I'm slow,
Make me quick to learn,
The important things, <u>I NEED</u> to know.

I've wasted too much time,
Now time has slipped me by.
Show me Lord, to better use my life,
That I may shine brighter, in your eye.

In Love
~Michael~

3/16/07   **Help Me See**

Please help me see,
Your love for me.

To know you're there,
And that you care.

Guide me safe and hold me near,
Take away my earthly fear.

Let me see, how I should be,
Rain down your love, so heavenly.

Let my heart be filled,
With your love,
Bring me, your trust, your faith,
And your strength, from above.

Help me see Lord,
So I'm no longer blind.
I want to get ahead in life,
I'm tired of being behind.

In Love
~Michael~

9/7/07　　**I'm Learning So Much**

I'm learning so much,
Continue to teach me,
Increase my strength,
And hold me closely;

That I may see,
What you want me to do,
As success comes my way,
I lift it to you.

Dear Father I am ready,
To be who you need,
I feel that from within,
You've planted a new seed.

As you teach me,
I want to continue to learn,
Establishing right from wrong,
I now do well, to discern.

I now want to learn,
And have opened my ears,
Some would say to me,
Why did it take so many years?

In Love,
~ Michael ~

9/17/07   **I Feel Your Strength**

I feel your strength today.
I feel your presence near.
You said you're here to stay,
You've made that very clear.

My prayers go to you,
And they need your touch,
Your guidance and love,
Are needed so much.

I'm breaking away,
From my thoughts of old,
Success awaits me,
As my hands, you hold.

I'm anxious to break free,
From the past of bad,
That behavior gained no good,
It only, made those close to me sad.

I now feel your forgiveness,
Your love and your strength,
To become more Christlike,
I will go to great length.

In Love
~Michael~

9/28/07 **I'm Beginning To See**

I'm beginning to see,
What you need of me.

To keep my eyes open and looking up,
And drink from life's over flowing cup.

To understand, it is in your time and not mine,
Until then, I'll enjoy each days sunshine.

For me to trust and see your way,
I'll keep my faith, beginning today.

It's now my time, for the past to go,
Keeping the future insight, is best I know.

I'm beginning to see,
It's important to be;

Christlike and caring,
For ME, this may be daring.

In Love
~Michael~

10/5/07   **Forgiving...**

Forgiving is a gift,
It's a tough one to give,
But we must do this,
All the days that we live.

We are only human,
And we will make mistakes,
Promising, not to do them again,
Is the beginning, of what it takes.

Forgiving our past,
Takes a strong fortitude,
Not forgiving, the past,
Is what, we should elude.

I want to make love to you,
In the downpour, of the rain,
I want to ignite, the embers, of love,
That in you, do remain.

I've never known,
A love so deep, and so pure,
It is my hope, my faith, and my love for you,
That tells me this, for sure.

You Can't Change
The *TRUTH*
But, The *TRUTH,*
Can Change . . .
YOUR LIFE . . .
It's *SIMPLE!*

We as one, can conquer all,
In good times and in bad,
Together we rise,
Never more, being sad.

I watch the sunrise,
And I watch the sunset,
And I think to myself... I wish my Polly was here,
I'm still in love with her yet.

But it is through these times,
That I see the light,
And I know no doubt,
That my love for you, is right.

I don't know why,
I can't let go,
It must be because... Where your heart is,
My heart, wants to follow.

In Love,
~ Michael ~

10/12/07   **Dear Lord I look To You**

My Dear Lord,
I look to you,
To strengthen me,
And guide me too.

Your love for me,
Has shown so bright,
My old ways were wrong,
My new Christlike ways, are right.

My thanks to you, O Lord,
In oh so many ways,
I look ahead with excitement,
To abundant and prosperous days.

I'm becoming more of the person,
You want me to be,
It's with new Christlike vision,
My eyes, are now able to see.

In Love,
~ Michael ~

10/29/07 Today I Give You Thanks

Today I give you thanks,
For all that you have done,
I look to you, for love and grace,
So my family, will be one.

All my thanks,
Goes from me to you,
You guide, you love,
And forgive me too.

It's the way,
It should be done,
And how this battle,
Will be won.

With great thanks,
Please bring me through,
Grant me, your favor,
In all that I do.

Today I give you thanks,
And I can't thank you enough,
You show me, how to make my life easy,
When I insist, on making it tough.

In Love
~Michael~

11/9/07   **Love You More Each Day**

My Dear Lord,
I love you more each day,
I see your ways at work,
Every time I pray.

It's like you,
Is how I wish to be,
Please strengthen my faith;
In rebuilding my family and me.

You guide, you love,
You watch from above.

I kneel to you, and look up and see,
The beauty you've created, all around me.

I thank you Lord,
For all you do,
My heart is yours,
It's my gift to you.

In Love,
~ Michael ~

11/22/07 **Remember To Give Thanks (Thanksgiving)**

Saying thanks is easy to do,
You say it to me, I say it to you.

Thanks goes a long way and pays dividends,
More importantly, think of the message it sends.

The cooking, the eating, the big football game,
There are no two Thanksgivings, ever the same.

After the feast and the days events are done,
Take time to give thanks, you're a fortunate one.

Yes, things can always be better,
But they also can be worse,
Be thankful, for what you have,
And **memorize**, this next verse.

"Thanksgiving is a time, to reflect and to see,
To be thankful, for all, our friends and family,
Be kind, and patient, with the ones we love,
And most of all, don't forget…
To THANK the good Lord above"

In Love,
~ Michael ~

12/30/07   **Today I See Clear**

Today I see clear,
Your vision, I hold near.

With your guidance I'll succeed,
In my life, your wisdom I need.

In this upcoming 2008,
I will no longer wait.

To move forward, and understand your will,
There's no time for mediocrity, no time to stand still.

You said,
My time was near,
I'm ready Lord,
To proceed without fear.

To do your will,
And do it right,
I will not give up,
To the end, I will fight.

I believe, you have chosen me,
To heal what I have done,
And this I will do, not alone,
But together with you, as one.

In Love,
~ Michael ~

1/3/08   **Let Me See**

Let me see,
<u>WHO</u> I need to be,
To receive your blessing,
For eternity.

Let me see,
<u>WHAT</u> you'll have me do,
Then give me the strength,
To see it through.

Let me see,
<u>WHEN</u> I go off track,
You'll lend a hand,
To guide me back.

Let me see,
<u>WHERE</u> you want me to be,
Keep me close,
Make it clear to me,

Let me see,
<u>WHY</u> I need to believe,
To keep my faith strong,
So your love I'll receive.

Let me see,
<u>HOW</u> you need me to be,
Protect me from the evil one,
Bring me closer, to your Son.

In Love,
~ Michael ~

1/30/08   I'm Learning To Think

I'm learning to think,
In a way that I should
Moving, in the right direction,
That's healthy and good.

There is some doubt,
About what I see,
But trust in me Lord,
It's not you, it's me.

I look to you,
To guide me well,
That one day my story,
Will be good enough to tell.

Beginning now and going forward,
I want to get it right,
In hopes that you,
Will keep me in your sight.

A new prosperous career,
I need real fast,
I pray to you Lord,
A long time, this one will last.

In Love,
~ Michael ~

2/21/08   **What I Need To See**

Guide me to those places, to what I need to see,
So that I may understand, what it is, you want of me.

I look to you, to guide me through;
The cloudiness of some days, and through my minds, confusion and haze.

Open my eyes, to see the light,
Guide my thoughts, from wrong to right.

To experience your love, make my vision clear,
That I may trust, that you are near.

I'm slow to learn, sometimes you see;
Be patient with me Lord, for after all, you made me.

I'm ready to become, the person you need me to be.
Please clear my mind and eyes, that I might see;
The abundant and prosperous future, you have planned for me.

In Love
~Michael~

3/15/08   **Father Please Guide Me**

Father please guide me,
And show me how,
To go forward in life,
Change my thoughts now.

I'm trying hard, to break old ways,
I'm looking ahead, to brighter days.

Through you I now know,
It's how it will be done,
Asking you to show me how,
Is decision #1

Be clear with me, without a doubt,
From you I need, your guidance pouring out.

I ask you Father, to show me how,
To be the person, I need to be now.

I'm listening Father, speak to me loud,
Make it clear to me, I want you to be proud.

In Love,
~ Michael ~

4/1/08   **New Chapter**

Today's the day,
That's big for me,
It begins a new chapter,
In my life's history.

It's you I seek,
To guide me through,
We make a great team,
That's me and you.

My test today,
I need a good grade,
I left who I was,
A new person of me, you've made.

My faith you have,
And everything inside,
I'm here because of you,
I longer choose to hide.

My mind is open,
My heart is alive,
I'm ready my Lord,
For my life to thrive.

I thank you my Father,
When you call me, my Son,
It is YOU, I want to please,
When my day is done.

In Love
~Michael~

4/7/08   **Make The Right Decisions**

Please make sure, I make the right decisions,
In all you'll have me do.
I'm tired Lord, I need your help,
I'm praying, you'll see me through.

Father guide me to the things,
You need for me to see,
Let me know what it is,
You need for me to be.

I'm ready Lord, I'm ready Lord,
To make the changes now,
I'm ready Lord, I promise Lord,
Please just show me how.

I trust in you, will all my heart,
With everything I know,
I trust in you, with all my heart,
The answers to me, I'll know you'll show.

In Love,
~ Michael ~

4/18/08 **You Won't Give Up**

You won't give up,
Even when I give in.
You always forgive,
When I seem to sin.

I still go wrong,
From time to time,
But you say to me, "my son, I love you,
I promise, you'll be fine".

I love you Lord,
And thank you much.
I long to have,
Your special touch.

I know I'm growing,
In a way you need.
I'm trying hard,
To plant the right seed.

Keep guiding me Lord,
I'm starting to see;
The things, that should've always,
Been important to me.

In Love,
~ Michael ~

44

4/30/08   **I Ask In Prayer**

I ask in prayer,
And you are there.

I stumble and fall,
You don't mind at all.

You help me up,
So that I may see,
You're always there,
Watching over me.

I need your guide,
To find my way,
You say, "trust in me,
And all will be okay".

It's ME, I doubt, not YOU, you see,
In spite of that, you'll rescue me.

I love you Lord, with all my heart,
Please, don't ever let us be apart.

In Love
~Michael~

5/27/08 **Broken Through**

I believe Lord,
I've broken through,
And I know,
I owe it all to you.

Bestow upon me, your faith, understanding;
Your wisdom and grace,
So that, when you think of me,
I might bring a smile, to your face.

Breaking through,
Has not been easy for me,
A bit slow I've been,
That, I know you see.

But I know, you're there watching,
And guiding me, as I walk,
The next step, is a new one,
I need to listen, instead of talk.

In Love
~Michael~

7/4/08   **Thank You For Your Patience**

I thank you, for your patience,
And your loving touch,
You have taught me well,
And I thank you much.

My eyes have been opened,
To see new ways,
I pray to you often,
To improve my days.

I trust in you Lord,
Because I know of your might,
I ask you dear Father,
Keep me from wrong, and move me to right.

Watch over me and guide me,
And help see me through,
I'm committed to getting better;
And following you.

In Love,
~ Michael ~

8/7/08   **You've Blessed Me**

You've blessed me,
Over and over again,
Despite the number,
Of times I sin.

I walk the path,
That is the right one now,
You always, bring me to the right place,
But I don't know why or how.

I'm thankful, for all you do,
I give you, all the praise,
And my eyes to you, I raise.

I owe everything to you;
My Mind,
My Body,
My Soul
My Spirit
My Heart
YOU and I, let's never be apart.

In Love,
~ Michael ~

8/31/08   **Guide Me In Your Way**

Guide me in your way,
So it's clear for me to see,
Help me understand,
How you need me to be.

Guide me to what it is Lord,
That you'll have me do,
I'll do my best, I promise Lord,
My best, is reserved for you.

I thank you Lord,
With all my heart,
From you,
Never let me, be apart.

As you guide me, in your way,
My heart and spirit, will be changed,
It is time, my thoughts and actions,
By you, are better rearranged.

In Love
~Michael~

9/7/08   **Guide Me To Strength**

Guide me to strength,
Guide me to light,
Guide me to know,
How to make things right.

Guide me to strength,
To the things you need me to do,
Bring back my wife, to be as one,
Instead of this, divided two.

I ask this of you,
From a deep inside love,
I've made a mess of things here,
Please guide me to strength from above.

In Love
~Michael~

9/12/08   I Received Your Message

I received,
Your message today,
About chillin' out,
And enjoying your way.

I've been uptight,
For too long now,
I'm opening my mind,
So you can show me how.

To date, yes,
I've been uptight,
Being caught up in me,
Instead of you, which is right.

I'm sorry Lord,
I will change my ways,
This will allow you, to bring me,
To brighter days.

In Love
~Michael~

51

9/29/08   **Blessed**

To be blessed is a gift, a gift from above,
You've been blessed, with the best gift,
The gift of your family's love.

You give unselfishly, to everyone, you're so special, to us all,
There is no task, to great for you,
No favor, too small.

You give of yourself, to those in need,
Your unselfish effort, is a blessing to us, indeed.

You are a man of great fortune, I know you realize,
The fortune you have, is you're blessed, in God's eyes.

God gave you a family, that comes together in love,
And it is, by HIS grace,
HE guides them, from above.

You bring joy & love to many, and are blessed, I know you see,
Though we, haven't talked much about it,
You, have inspired me.

You know, you're loved deeply, you're known as, Gran'pa Dick & Dad,
As I write this, my tears do flow, you're the Dad, I never had.

I love you with all my heart, God Bless You.
(In Honor of Dick Donnelly)

In Love,
~ Michael ~

9/30/08   I Am Ready For Your Help

You Can't Change
The *TRUTH*,
But, The *TRUTH*,
Can Change . . .
YOUR *LIFE* . . .
It's *SIMPLE*!

I'm ready for your help,
Yes, stubborn I can be,
But you've known this for some time,
Throughout my history.

That's no excuse,
For things I have done,
Confessing to you Lord,
Has lifted, from me a ton.

I'm ready for your help,
But I feel too guilty to ask,
Making me Christlike,
Will be no easy task.

But I know this one thing,
I'm done, with my selfish ways,
Please change me lord, I really want this,
But don't take too many days.

In Love
~ Michael ~

10/16/09   **Be Patient With Me**

Be Patient with me,
And show me your way.
It's been a long time coming,
That I'm in this place today.

Thank you, Lord Jesus,
For your faithful unity today,
To show my love, and trust in you,
I make the needed changes you say.

I love you Father,
You've been gracious to forgive,
Your spirit is alive in me,
And now, it's my turn to give.

Please guide me Father,
I can't do this alone,
I've been away a long time,
Please show me the way home.

In Love
~Michael~

2/3/09   **My Dearest Father**

My Dearest Father,
Guide me well,
I've been a bit off balance,
I'm sure you can tell.

I need help now,
In a very big way,
If you would be so kind,
Please start today.

I find myself down,
Way too much,
I desperately need,
Your loving touch.

Please help me Father,
And help me soon,
I feel my life,
Has gone to ruin.

I know my best days,
Are still in front of me,
I ask you, my dear friend,
Keep my eyes open, so these days I can see.

In Love
~Michael~

3/3/09   **I Feel You In My Life**

I feel you in my life,
Please guide me in your way,
Fill my heart and life with strength,
So my ChristLikeness, grows each day.

You are my Father,
Please forgive me, for what I have done,
I want to change from being;
A disappointing son.

I know, I'm getting better,
I've gained some strength, that's true,
But it is only through forgiving me,
That I grow, to be more like you.

In Love,
~ Michael ~

3/17/09   **I Ask Your Help**
             (Happy St. Paddy's Day!)

I ask your help,
And you're always there,
I feel your guidance,
And your love, you do share.

Give it to you, you say,
And worry me no more,
Trust in you, you say,
And worries go out the door.

I look to you,
For guidance and grace,
But frustration appears,
All around my face.

Help me Father,
With your strength and love,
And open my ears,
To your words from above.

I ask your help,
Because I don't know;
How to give love like you,
That you, are so gracious to show.

In Love
~Michael~

4/2/09　　**To Use My Time**

I need your help, to use my time,
The way you need me to,
I fall short, too often Lord,
When it comes to seeing you.

My rhymes are off sometimes,
But they're very meaningful,
I try to behave, the way I should,
Not like the, "China Shop Bull".

I'm searching Lord every day,
To be the person you want me to be,
I need to be better here and now,
While keeping my eye on eternity.

I love you with my heart and soul,
And ask you every day,
Help me see, what I need to do,
Then lead me all the way.

In Love
~Michael~

4/26/09   **Thank You For Listening**

Thank you for listening,
Though you're not obligated to,
I ask, for guidance and wisdom,
And it must, come from you.

I strive to get better,
To discern right from wrong,
I hope my path, to learning is short,
But my journey through life, is long.

I love you my Father,
Please show me the way,
Your wisdom of tomorrow,
Is needed today.

I ask to be guided,
Because I am lost,
I ask for my family's return,
I commit to you, at all cost.

I know you hear, what I'm asking,
And I'm sure, you've answered me,
But Remember I'm only human,
You might need to tell me, "times three."

In Love,
~ Michael ~

5/19/09   **Please Hear My Prayers**

Please hear my prayers,
And answer as you need,
As my time grows short,
It is time, I must heed.

I promise Lord,
I am now a better man,
One who wants healing,
And to clearly understand.

With my vision O Lord,
I have been blind to see,
Please make it clear,
It's been very cloudy for me.

Deliver me Father,
To the place I need to be,
I'm anxious to get there,
Please bless me, abundantly.

In Love,
~ Michael ~

6/24/09   You've Opened My Eyes

You've opened my eyes,
To a new way of listening today,
I must change my words,
To reflect what I say.

I've learned a few things,
In which I'm afraid of,
I need to listen intently,
And show unselfish love.

You've opened my eyes,
So that I could see,
To close my mouth, and open my ears,
To hear what you're telling me.

The hurt I feel,
Must go away,
And be replaced,
For the things I pray.

Please Dear Lord,
Help me to change today,
And have me behave,
In your preferred way.

In Love,
~ Michael ~

6/29/09   **I'm Grateful**

Please know I'm grateful,
For all that you do,
I act more like me,
Instead of, more like you.

I'm grateful for your guidance, your love,
And your touch,
You've showed me, it's important to love,
And to love, very much.

The tears I cry,
Confuse me they do,
I don't know what they're for,
My sins, my gratefulness, or for hurting you.

I'm ready Lord,
To be that person, you need me to be,
Take my hand and lead me there,
I'm still too blind, to see.

In Love
~Michael~

7/16/09   **Thanks**

Dear Lord, thank you,
For all you do,
For bringing me to a place,
To better understand you.

I thank you for your forgiveness,
Your protection and your love.
I couldn't become the person you need,
Without your watchful eye from above.

I've never been more grateful,
For the patience and guidance you show.
The need to repay you is present,
That I would like you to know.

I'm excited about improving,
And leaving my old ways behind,
I want to keep moving forward,
Never having to rewind.

In Love
~Michael~

7/21/09   **Now**

Now is the time to begin,
No more waiting and sitting,
Feel the drive from within.

Let the Lord guide you,
Open up to his ways,
You'll be amazingly surprised,
At the dividends He pays.

Get moving now,
Take action my friend,
Do the things YOU need to do,
Don't wait, to begin the mend.

The time is upon you,
Yes it is now,
If you're not sure what to do,
Just ASK THE LORD HOW.

In Love
~Michael~

7/29/09   **Marriage**

Marriage is a gift,
Not for one, but for two,
It's God's way of sharing his love,
From His heart with you.

It's a union for life,
To have and to hold,
It's a bond of love,
Now as you are young and as you grow old.

You are joined in Marriage,
Because you're in love,
Keep God in your life,
He'll guide you from above.

It's a joyous time, for song, dance and smiles,
Stay true to each other,
Through the storms,
And over life's, sometimes rough miles.

Be true to each other,
Trust in God's power,
Look into each other's eyes,
Each day, each minute, each hour.

You Can't Change
The *TRUTH,*
But, The *TRUTH,*
Can Change . . .
YOUR LIFE
It's *SIMPLE!*

Give each other kindness, respect and love,
All the days of your lives,
Be a faithful example,
To other, Husbands and Wives.

Marriage is a commitment,
Of mind, soul and heart,
Be sure to give of yourself,
It's not science, but a practiced art.

Don't take your commitment lightly,
Stay true to your love, and nurture each other,
Be selfless in your love,
Don't be distracted, by any other.

Share your happiness with many,
Care for each other in loving ways,
Keep God in the center of your heart,
You'll be blessed abundantly, for all your Married days.

In Love,
~ Michael ~

8/13/09   **Beginning To Understand**

Thanks to you Lord,
I'm beginning to understand,
Thanks for reaching out to me,
And extending your loving hand.

It's taken a while,
For me to see,
What my Life's direction,
Really needs to be.

I pray and listen,
But don't always hear,
Somehow I'm Feeling,
What you need from me is near.

My mind is open,
My heart and spirit too,
I'm beginning to understand,
It's not about me, It's all about you.

I say I'm ready Lord,
I hope you feel that way too,
I know you'll agree, my understanding,
Is long overdue.

In Love,
~ Michael ~

8/18/09   **Aware**

I've become aware of you,
In my life more each day,
I'm starting to live my life,
In a more Christ-like way.

Listen to my heart Lord,
As it reaches out to you,
Fill me with your strength Lord,
To do the things you need me to.

My thoughts are challenged,
But now, I'm more aware,
When I call to you,
I'm beginning to see you there.

I'm more aware than ever,
But I've still a long way to go,
If the time comes when I stumble,
You'll steady me, I know

In Love
~Michael~

8/24/09   **Opening My Eyes**

Lord I'm beginning,
To open my eyes to see,
Just what it is,
You need me to be.

I'm weak you see Lord,
I need your guide,
What I need to be, is in me,
But buried deep inside.

I want to break through,
But what holds me back,
Is that the enemy,
Is on the constant attack.

Be with me Lord,
So I will win,
The enemy makes it,
Too easy to sin.

So guard me Lord,
And see me through,
Because after all,
I need to be more like you.

In Love
~Michael~

9/1/09   **In Losing Someone,**
          We Find Something

When someone leaves us,
It can make us sad.
Many emotions rise up,
From anger, maybe peace or being mad.

This is when we must stop and think,
Life goes by so quickly, it could pass in an eye's blink.

It's at this time, we need to slow down and observe,
And ask ourselves, am I doing my best to love and to serve.

When we lose someone, there's something to be found,
Fond memories should rise and abound.

Not all memories will be loving and good,
But when a loved one passes, all ill will should.

Remember, be slow to anger and quick to forgive,
For it is only this one life, we all have to live.

Imagine for a moment, you knew the day you would die,
Would you act differently, and live life with a gleam in your eye.

We don't know our day of passing,
But we all know, that day will come,
So take this time, to make amends,
Heal all wounds, not just some.

When someone we love leaves us,
We experience the void of their touch,
If I only had more time with them,
I could've, I would've, is said way too much.

When we lose someone, something is found,
We realize a part of us, is no longer around.

Here's an important message for all of us to hear,
Love and make peace, with the people near and dear.

In Love,
~ Michael ~

9/23/09   **Open Your Mind**

An open mind,
Must be clear,
In order to feel,
The Lord is near.

An open mind,
Lets blessings take hold,
It lets new thinking in,
And moves out the old.

It's easy to do,
If you just take the time,
The choice is yours,
And the choice is mine,

The Lord will visit you,
In your times of need,
He'll plant within you,
The appropriate seed.

Cultivate and nurture that seed,
To grow the right way,
Always keep your faith strong,
And follow the Lord's way.

In Love,
~ Michael ~

9/29/09   **Hope**

The thing about hope,
It's free to us all,
No matter how big,
No matter how small.

You can choose to have it,
Or give it away,
Combine hope with faith,
And you'll strengthen each day.

Hope is a small word,
But it packs a lot of power,
Ask the Lord to <u>highlight</u> your Hope,
Every minute, every second, every hour.

When you feel all hope is lost,
And the journey seems too long,
Tell the Lord, you need some help,
And his love, will keep you strong.

In Love,
~ Michael ~

10/12/09   **My Heart**

My heart is hurt Lord,
Will it ever heal,

I pray it will Lord,
And I ask as I kneel.

I wish things were different,
The one I love is gone,

My friends tell me "give up,
It's time to move on".

It's easier said than done O Lord,
I try to move forward every day,

Living in the past, is not where I want to be,
Bring someone now I pray.

Keep on, keeping on,
Is what I need to do,

Today, I thought of her way too much,
Lord please guide me, it's up to you.

In Love
~Michael~

10/20/09   **Listen**

Open my ears,
For me to hear;
The words from your lips;
That are near and dear.

I try to listen,
But I'm impatient you see,
I need answers now,
Please listen to, and answer me.

I know, I know,
It's in your time they'll come,
But please, I feel lost,
Can you give me some?

Thank you Father,
For your patience with me,
I'll continue to listen and wait,
For your answers to see.

I don't always listen,
I want the quick fix,
But like hands on the clock,
Your hands too, move with deliberate ticks.

In Love
~Michael~

11/23/09   **Wisdom**

Wisdom is something,
We all search to acquire,
Remember it's a blessing,
While pursuing it, never tire.

The older we get,
The wiser we become,
Not true of all,
But it is for some.

Wisdom has a cost,
At different levels we pay,
At what price do we acquire wisdom,
Is the game we must play.

Understanding breeds wisdom,
So listen then you'll know,
How to gain and keep wisdom,
And share it where you go.

Keep your mind open,
To God's wise ways and you'll see,
Wisdom will come to you,
Then cherish it, abundantly.

In Love
~Michael~

12/1/09   **Moving Forward**

Moving forward,
Is what we should do.
When we experience something,
That has made us feel blue.

Remembering what happened,
Is okay to a degree,
But not if it blocks,
Your future vision to see.

Hurt goes deep,
When someone leaves,
But as we move forward,
The pain will ease.

Have faith in yourself,
And the good Lord above,
Ask Him to hear you,
And give you His love.

It takes great strength,
To let someone or something go,
But once you're mind moves forward,
Your heart, is sure to follow,

In Love
~Michael~

12/8/09   **Kevin D**

Kevin D is a friend of mine,
A special light around him, does shine.

He's always there for a friend,
And how he'll help you, there's no end.

He's strong and faithful,
And refuses to quit,
He's bound and determined,
This cancer he'll whip.

Today we laughed,
And "HE," made "ME," feel good,
He said to me, "lighten up and laugh,
For every day of life is good".

He's more concerned for others,
Than he is for himself.
That's what makes him and his wife Mandy,
In my book, top shelf.

Kevin is a fighter,
But not in the outward sense,
His faith in a better spiritual life,
Is amazingly immense.

(For my dear friend Kevin DiGiammarino)

In Love
~Michael~

12/10/09   **The Past**

The past is the past,
You must let it go,
"Trust in the Lord",
He says it is so.

We hold on too long,
To things that are gone.

Look forward my friend,
To the beginning not the end.

Doors have been opened,
For you to walk through,
Have faith in the Lord,
It's expected of you.

If you're not sure what to do,
Ask the Lord He'll guide you.

But know this and be assured,
Your faith will be secured.

The Lord will provide protection,
And victory for all, you've endured.

In Love
~Michael~

12/15/09   **Our Time Here**

Our time here,
Is not determined by us,
So use it wisely my friend,
And over trivial things, do not fuss.

Learn to laugh and love,
Every day,
Because when today is gone,
Don't be sorry, okay?

We want to get better,
At the things we do,
Improve your friendships,
And it will improve you.

You need to use your time,
To improve your talents to your best,
Our Lord above is our teacher,
He wants you to "Ace", your life's test.

In Love
~Michael~

12/21/09   Hung By My Tongue

Hung by my tongue,
Is what happened today,
I tried to be quiet,
But something stupid, I had to say.

Just zip my lip,
And all would have been fine,
But I opened my dumb mouth,
And out flowed, not so brilliant words of mine.

When will my brain,
And mouth agree,
Some words are best left unsaid,
Instead of flowing free.

Being hung by my tongue,
Too often happens to me,
I want more love in my words,
Much more frequently.

Say your words wisely,
For once you give them, they're gone forever,
Give people kind words,
And regrets, you'll have them never.

In Love
~Michael~

1/4/10   **New Beginnings**

It's new beginnings,
When great faith takes place,
Remember life is a marathon,
Not a quick sprint race.

Continuous improvement,
Is what God asks of us,
Not dwelling on past mistakes,
It's definitely a must.

Anything new in the beginning,
Is usually pleasant and fun,
But the race is not always easy,
It takes perseverance to be won.

In new beginnings,
There's a new chance to get it right,
Be determined to have victory,
Ask God's help, every morning, noon, and night.

In Love,
~ Michael ~

1/26/10   **Healing**

Healing is important,
And it comes in many ways,
Healing from a hurt,
May take a few, or many days.

Hurt can hold us back from growing,
We must open ourselves to heal,
A good way to begin this journey,
Ask for God's help, as we kneel.

We can't do it all at once,
If help is needed, you must ask,
Have faith and persistence my friend,
For God, there is no tough task.

People will hurt you,
Whether you let them or not,
Just know, that with prayers to God,
This gives healing, your best shot.

In Love,
~ Michael ~

2/26/10   **Meeting Again**

When you've not seen someone,
For a very long time,
Then you bump into them,
For no reason or rhyme;

Ask yourself, why now and why them,
What is it we're supposed to do.
Is the Lord working on us,
That will create something new.

That was the Lord at work,
He wanted you there at that time,
He works in mysterious ways,
Not always obvious, sometimes sublime.

Be glad He's there,
To guide you through,
Enjoy your time together,
Now ask the Lord, what should you do?

In Love
~Michael~

3/1/10   **Let The Lord In**

Let the Lord in,
And you will see,
How quickly he'll raise you,
To your next victory.

Stop trying to do it,
All by yourself,
Try putting your pride and ego,
Up on the shelf.

He sees what you need,
And He's ready to show;
You your dreams and your wishes,
Do you deserve them, He'll know.

The Lord listens,
And He hears very well,
Now you be still and you listen,
And to you He will tell;

The things that are needed,
For you to do,
Don't force the lord's timing,
It will come, in His time to you.

In Love
~Michael~

3/10/10   **When You Want To Quit**

When you want to quit,
And things aren't going your way,
Get on your knees, put hands together,
And say help me Lord, as you pray.

Anyone can quit,
It's the champions and winners that say,
This is only one season of my life,
And my winning time is on its way.

The Lord sees what's happening,
Stay strong in your faith and believe,
For those who fight the good fight of faith,
The Lord is preparing, great things to receive.

Don't be shy, ask for help,
And it will come today,
For when you ask the Lord to guide you,
Remember, He is The Truth, The Love, The Light, and The Way.

In Love,
~ Michael ~

3/13/10   **A Time To Let Go**

You will know,
When it's time to let go.

Yes, it's hard to understand,
The feeling's at hand.

You try to hold on,
To someone from the past,
If only you would ask God to help,
And put him first and not last.

He will show you what to do,
If you'll trust and let go,
Who do you think has the answers?
My money's on God, to know.

When it's tough letting go,
Of that very special one,
Say hey, help me out Lord,
I know, you can get it done.

When it's time, you'll tell me;
What needs to be done.
I will dare to let go;
Because your way is the one.

In Love
~Michael~

3/30/10   **Being Thankful**

Being thankful is something;
We all need to do.
There are many things in life,
That makes this important for you.

Being thankful in good times,
And challenging times too,
It's these seasons of your life,
That builds the true character in you.

Being thankful for all things in life,
Makes us aware of blessings and needs;
Knowing that down deep in our hearts,
Make the time to plant thankful seeds.

Being thankful now for all we have,
It could all be gone tomorrow,
But if you've given thanks today,
There'll be no need for any sorrow.

In Love,
~ Michael ~

4/10/10   **Trust In The Lord**

Trust in the Lord,
And you will see,
How much clearer,
Your path will be.

Don't try to solve things on your own,
Trust in the Lord and let them go.
Times like these will test your faith,
Learn to push aside your ego.

Trust in the Lord,
He'll get it done,
Take action guided by Him,
You'll be the happier one.

When someone you love,
Betrays your trust,
Tell the Lord that it hurts,
Your healing is a must.

After all, who do you think knows best?
It is in He, that we'll find our rest.

In Love,
~ Michael ~

4/14/10   **Blessings**

Blessings come to us, in many ways,
We receive many blessings, in many days.

We're not always aware,
Of the blessings we see,
They may be right in front of us,
It could be YOU, or it could be ME.

Blessings surround us every day,
We experience blessings in every way.

From health and families,
And abundance of life,
Even from challenges,
That cause us strife.

In our lives,
There are many things,
It's the joy we experience,
That this blessing brings.

Our Minds, Our Hearts, Our Spirits, Our Eyes,
Must be open at all times,
To see the Lord's surprise.

In Love,
~ Michael ~

5/3/10   **Open Your Heart**

Open your heart,
So you can hear,
That the Lord our God,
Is very near.

He longs to hold you,
And keep you secure,
This way you'll know,
You're safe for sure.

He knows your heart,
Has hope and desire,
He's here you know,
To stoke your spiritual fire.

Trust in Him,
And open your heart,
Let him inside,
So your, bountiful future can start.

In Love,
~ Michael ~

5/13/10   **Confused**

I'm confused but must move forward,
In my actions, thoughts and heart,
This is why I come to you,
A new life, I must start.

Please clear my confusion,
And make me strong.
Let me accept your plan for me,
As I should've all along.

I need your guidance Lord,
To help me to break through,
All my love, faith, and trust, my Lord,
Is all dependent upon you.

I'm so confused Lord,
Help me see your way,
Lead me by your hand Lord,
On your brightly lit path today.

Please clear all my confusion,
No more confusion to be had,
Today I start seeing clearer
Clearer than I ever have.

In Love
~Michael~

5/13/10   **Help Me Today**

Help me today Lord,
I'm frustrated and I don't know why.
Please enlighten me to what to do,
I'm frustrated, but I refuse to cry.

This uneasiness I'm feeling,
Is completely misunderstood,
I'm letting my emotions, get the best of me,
Instead of controlling them like I should.

Help me today with my frustration,
It's coming from my heart,
I'm feeling this way because,
My heart has been torn apart.

These feelings still linger inside me.
My divorce was 4 years ago,
But forward looking my eyes must be,
Some days, it's still hard to let go.

Help me today Lord,
I'm ready to be healed,
That is why, I'm here today,
And before you, I have kneeled.

In Love,
~ Michael ~

6/8/10   **A Time For Change**

A time for change,
Will come you'll see,
A friend or foe,
What will you, let change be.

Change at first,
May be hard to understand,
If that is the case,
Ask God to take your hand.

With open heart, mind and eyes,
Something awesome you might see,
Change could make, YOU;
Into that person, you NEED to be.

When change happens,
You get to decide,
To take advantage of the change,
Or withdraw and hide.

If you're still afraid of change,
And it might scare you too,
Just ask the Lord to show you the way,
He's promises, to lead you through.

In Love
~ Michael ~

7/19/10   **Worrying**

Worrying,
Is something we all do,
We all would like to stop,
But don't know how to.

We're only human,
And FACTS, we have that's true,
The Lord tells us often,
Worrying is for Him, and not for you.

Easier said than done we say,
It's a healthier way to live,
By worrying, does you no good, says the Lord,
So your worrying, to Him, you should give.

I say please help me Lord,
Set my worries free,
But the more I worry,
The more they cling to me.

Please forgive me Lord for worrying,
And take my worries away,
You alone my Lord,
Can set me free, from my worries today.

In Love,
~ Michael ~

You Can't Change
The *TRUTH,*
But, The *TRUTH,*
Can Change . . .
YOUR LIFE . . .
It's *SIMPLE*!

8/2/10   **Tired**

I'm tired of being tired,
I need all this pain to end,
There are important things in life,
In which I need to attend.

I'm sad and distracted,
When things need to be done,
I need some help from somebody,
I pray Jesus is the one.

I've been down too long,
Don't know how much more I can take,
Please Dear Lord rescue me,
A happy person of me, please make.

I hurt from past transgressions,
Please lift this pain from me,
I strive to be on track,
But this seems too distant to see.

I want to be a great person,
One that does right by thee,
Please, please, help me Lord,
I want to be, hap-py.

In Love
~Michael~

8/4/10   **Learning / How We Learn**

We learn, when we're young,
It comes in many ways,
We learn, when we're old,
Some learning goes with passing days.

We learn, when things happen to us,
Sometimes we don't know how,
We just accept it for awhile,
And take the learning for now.

Then we question,
Why did that happen to me?
We try to understand,
And ask, is this just my destiny?

We get confused and concerned,
And say, I don't understand,
Then we get upset and say,
The answers, I demand!

When all else fails,
And frustration kicks in,
Don't give up, keep on doing what you can,
And take your learning Him.

In Love,
~ Michael ~

8/8/10   **It's Time To Heal**

It's time to heal,
And forget the past,
Look forward my son,
Blessed days are ahead, I promise they'll last.

You're healing now,
You'll hurt no more,
I've open it, for you,
Now, walk through the door.

You've suffered long,
But you have learned much,
Keep an open mind, heart and spirit;
To my favor and my touch.

I've given you,
The strength you seek,
Be strong my son,
No more being weak.

I'm proud of you,
As a Father to a Son,
It's your time now,
Be the one I picked, to get it done.

In Love
~Michael~

8/16/10   **Listening To God**

Listening to God,
Is what we all should do,
It doesn't matter where or when,
But it does matter who.

Listen, be still and be quiet,
You'll hear the voice in your heart,
Don't wait till tomorrow to listen,
Today is the day to start.

Listen to God,
You'll hear amazing things,
Let God guide your ways,
It will lesson your stings.

Listen with your heart,
And not with your ears,
It's the spirit in your heart,
That knows God's voice, and hears.

Listen, to the one who loves,
And is reaching out to you,
No need to feel lonely anymore,
You'll be touched and feel new.

In Love
~Michael~

8/19/10   **Fresh Start**

To get a fresh start,
Is a gift from above,
It's one way the Lord rewards you,
For your kindness and your love.

A fresh start can be scary,
Because you're starting from square one,
Be thankful for this special chance,
That has come from God's son.

We all have done things,
That have hurt people in the past,
But commit to a better future,
And ask for God's help to last.

Starting fresh is a gift,
Not one should take lightly,
It will take perseverance,
But don't give up, ever so slightly.

Thank the Lord for your fresh start,
And get His help every day,
Always ask Him to guide you,
In His, very special way.

In Love
~Michael~

8/22/10   **Releasing The Hurt**

Releasing the hurt,
May take some time,
But this must be done,
To keep my life in line.

Release the hurt,
And live life anew,
I've been hurting for some time,
I miss the one love, that was true.

I'm ready to release the hurt,
And create for me a new mold.
I come to the chapel and bend my knees,
And prayerfully, my hands I fold.

How do I release the hurt?
How do I let my hurt go.

In a funny way, I say to myself,
The hurt is not worth it, just let go man! Let go!

The Lord promises me,
This hurt, I will no longer know.

The Lord says he'll guide me,
Just ask, and it is so.

He also says, *"Don't worry my son,
I'm always here for you, you know."*

In Love,
~ Michael ~

8/27/10   **Time To Get Going**

It's time to get going,
And forget about the past,
Shake it off and get it in gear,
You want first place, not last.

Let go of the junk,
That is holding you back,
Put energy into your skills,
Not the things you lack.

It's time to get going,
Be thankful for what you've got,
Stop dwelling on unimportant things,
And the things, you have not.

Use the blessings, God has given you,
Use them to <u>YOUR</u> best,
God will move you forward,
Away from the ones who rest.

It's hard to do it by yourself,
So get some help, from the Lord above,
He'll be quick to help, if you ask him right,
He'll help you, out of love.

In Love
~ Michael~

9/13/10   **Don't Stop Believing**

Don't stop believing,
At times you will,
When that time comes,
Pray harder still.

Belief is faith,
Down deep inside,
Let God know your fears,
From him, never should you hide.

Yes we are tested,
Most times, for our own good,
This, will bring us closer to God,
As the design, of his plan should.

Sure we get scared,
Sometimes we worry and stress,
But ask God to guide you,
You'll be uptight, a lot less.

Believe in your heart,
Open your spirit and mind,
God promises, if you have faith,
He'll not leave you behind.

In Love
~Michael~

10/17/10   **Acceptance**

Acceptance of things,
We do not know,
Can cause us stress,
But we must let that go.

Put your trust in the Lord,
He'll see you through,
Open yourself to new learning,
He'll calm your fears for you.

We hold on tight to acceptance,
In fear, we may lose it,
While all along when we could've,
We've never even used it.

Accepting things,
We don't understand,
This is called faith,
Put yourself in the Lord's hand.

Help me Father,
To accept and understand,
I feel shot up into the air,
Please help me, to softly land.

In Love
~Michael~

11/15/10 **Lord I Need Your Help**

Lord, I need your help,
To guide me from the past,
Clear these thoughts, from my mind,
I no longer want them to last.

My heart was hurt,
I need to heal,
I'm at the Adoration Chapel,
And Before you I kneel.

Please bring me peace,
To my spirit, mind and heart,
I long to be clear headed,
To be successful, at my fresh start.

Lord, I need your help to guide me,
And steer me, where you know,
If I'm sure it's you, that's pushing me,
I'll be more willing, to go.

Note…Lord, thanks for being patient with me.

In Love,
~ Michael ~

11/21/10 **Remember YOU
Are A Blessing**

Remember YOU are a blessing,
YOU were created by you know who,
The Lord has special things in store,
Especially designed for YOU.

YOU may be a Mom or YOU may be a Dad,
YOU may be a Friend or a Sister or Brother,
No matter what your role or relationship,
We need to help, love and guide one another.

YOU are a blessing,
And here to serve our Lord,
If you're not sure how to serve,
Ask Him, He'll keep YOU from being bored.

God gave this earth,
The gift of YOU,
God will help someone,
Help YOU, see it through.

But remember this,
With all His heart he loves YOU,
So when YOU ask for help,
Ask Him, what is it, YOU can do.

In Love
~Michael~

12/17/10   **Pain In My Heart**

Help me Father,
With the pain in my heart,
My new life's beginning,
And I'm scared to start.

Letting go of past pain,
Is hard for me to do,
Your message said to me today,
Let it go, I'll give, what is needed to you.

So I said I would;
Give my pain to you,
In doing this you promised me,
This is how you'd get me through.

I want to have this burden leave,
So I can move forward in my life,
I believe Lord you will do this,
Take away this stress and strife.

I feel your presence with me,
So I know, Your will be done.
I look to you to guide me Lord,
Because you are, God's chosen son.

In Love
~Michael~

2/22/11   **Turn It Over To God**

When you have done,
Everything you can do,
It's time to turn it over,
To you know who.

If you did your best,
To get it done,
Then turn it over,
To number one.

We can only do so much,
In our meager human ways,
Let the one, who can get it done,
Bring happiness to your days.

We can push and push,
And try and try,
But turn it over to God,
And you'll see why.

You will be more fulfilled,
And happier this way,
Turn it over to God,
And start trusting in him today.

In Love,
~ Michael ~

3/6/11   **Tears**

Not all tears,
Are bad,
There are happy ones,
And some that are sad.

People of all shapes and sizes,
Shed tears for many reasons,
Tears like life, they ebb and flow,
Through all, our many seasons.

Tears flow from our eyes,
And change with our emotions,
Sometimes our tears dry up,
Other times, they flow like oceans.

When our tears are done,
There's a hexing that we feel,
But all our tears are counted by God,
And he knows, your tears are real.

So don't stop your tears,
Let them out, and let them flow,
But remember this, God does see your tears,
He will comfort you, this you must know.

In Love
~Michael~

3/1/11   **Be Who You Are**

Did you ever feel,
You weren't good enough?
Swallowing your pride,
Can be kind of tough.

You try to be,
Like someone you know,
But be who you are,
From there you can grow.

Don't put on silly fake faces,
Be who you are, from your head,
Down to your shoe laces.

God made you to be,
Just who you are,
Don't mess with his creation,
By straying too far.

Use the gifts,
God has given to you,
Remember this, He purposely made one,
And not a duplicate of you.

In Love
~Michael~

3/26/11   **Feeling Confused**

I'm feeling confused,
And I don't know why,
I'm up then down,
And sometimes sigh.

I know I'm blessed,
And thankful for each day,
As I looked in the mirror,
To myself I did say;

"If you can't lift yourself up,
Ask God to show you how,
Then you'll see just by asking,
That God is present here and now.

You've been blessed with particular talents
And you have them for a reason,
Use them as God expects you to,
No matter, your personal season.

And always know,
God hears your prayer and intention,
Don't forget he loves you much,
This reminder, I had to mention.

In Love
~Michael~

4/11/11   **These Times Are Tough**

These times are tough,
Yes, sometimes they are,
So are you going to quit,
Or be a bright star.

Our seasons come,
And our seasons go,
Stay strong in your faith,
The tough times, will leave you know.

When something is tough,
Take care of it now,
It won't get the best of you,
Let God show you how.

Some times can be tough,
Just know they won't last,
Be a person of the present,
Not one who lives in the past.

Tough times will go,
Tough people will stay,
Remember, who put you here,
And look forward to a brighter day.

In Love
~Michael~

4/12/11   **A Time Of Thanks**

Give thanks each day,
For all God does for you,
A simple thank you Lord;
Will probably do.

Saying thanks, is a good place to start,
Be sincere and meaningful,
And say it from your heart.

The Lord loves to help you,
In the things you do each day,
When your way doesn't work,
Be different, try it His way.

It's amazing what will happen,
When you ask, please help me Lord today,
He'll reach out his hand, you'll feel his touch,
And now, you're on your way.

Take time to give thanks,
It's easy to do,
Simply say thank you Lord,
For blessing me, I really love you.

In Love
~Michael~

4/17/11   Time Passes Away

When time passes away, we can't get it back.
How time is used, is what keeps us on track.

Time taken for granted, is not wise, but a mistake.
Time can escape us, but not the decisions we make.

Time will pass as we must too,
Don't let time quickly pass by you.

As time passes away, don't watch it go by;
Use the time you have wisely, with a gleam in your eye;

It lessens the regrets and the "I'm sorry's', we say,
We wish we could change time and bring back, a happier day.

But now that you know time is precious and good;
Live life, as if it will be gone tomorrow, as you know you should.

Time passes slowly,
Sometimes it passes fast;
One thing that's assured, that times,
Be they good or bad, won't last.

Being a good steward of time;
Is what we need to know,
And showing kindness and love;
Is the way to go.

Remember, we do not own time,
It's only something we borrow,
Use time wisely,
That way there's little sorrow.

Time passes away before our eyes,
Time allows us to see our truths and lies.

If I only had more time we say,
I know I could make it right,
By then It's too late to make the change,
Begin now, to improve your spiritual sight.

In Love
~ Michael ~

4/26/11   **There Comes A Time**

There comes a time, in everyone's life;
They'll experience pain, and experience strife.

There comes a time, we'll need a friend,
They'll somehow bring; our strife to an end.

We lean on friends, when we're sad and blue.
There will come a time, when they'll be down;
And need a friend like you.
When that time comes
What will you choose to do?

Be a true and caring friend,
And do everything you can,
Or be fair weathered and absent,
And be too busy to lend a hand.

There's an old saying, that often does comes true,
What goes around, comes around,
What would you like to come to you?

There comes a time,
In our lives we'll see,
That we are all human and need help,
Be the best friend, you're able to be.

In Love
~Michael~

5/28/11 **Let The Hurt Go**

Let the hurt go;
It's the right thing, but hard to do
Whether it's intentional hurt or by mistake,
Don't let hurt consume you.

We begin to heal,
And try to forgive,
Let the hurt go,
And remain positive.

It's easier said than done,
Being forgiving, is what we must do,
Let the hurt go,
Jesus did this, for me & for you.

Let the hurt go,
Trust in me, Jesus said,
Ask for His guidance,
Then be still and be led.

It takes prayer and patience;
To let the hurt go,
Stay tuned into Jesus,
His help, He's ready to show.

In Love
~Michael~

6/2/11   **HE Is With You**

When life treats you,
A little rough,
HE is with you,
To make you tough.

HE's with you in sadness,
HE's with you in joy,
HE's been with you since you've been,
A little girl or little boy.

HE's with you when you're up,
HE's with you when you're down,
All he wants is your love,
So smile and don't frown.

HE's with you in the day,
HE's with you in the night,
HE's always there to protect you,
So there's no need for fright.

HE's there to love you,
And guide you all the way,
All you have to do, is trust Him,
And acknowledge Him each day.

In Love
~Michael~

6/20/11   **When I Didn't Think**
                I Was Good Enough

It all began,
When I was young,
The "you're not good enough" song,
My Mother had sung.

You're just like your Father,
And he's no good,
I thought, I don't know what you mean,
But I had wished that I could.

There was no encouragement,
She just didn't know how,
It wasn't her fault, it wasn't given to her,
I can clearly see that now.

I know she did the best she could,
I'm sure it was tough on her too;
Not to have the love from her family,
That she might have been due.

I've prayed long and hard,
To be able to understand,
I've now learned, to turn things over,
To God's, loving hand.

In Love
~Michael~

9/5/11   **Strengthen The Parts**
           Of Me That Are Weak

Dear Lord, I hear you speaking to me,
About the parts of me that are weak,
I can make them stronger,
But it's through you, my strength I must seek.

Inside I am strong,
But it doesn't always come through,
I pray to you my Father,
I gain my strength in you.

There are tears in my eyes,
And desires in my heart.
I miss the one I love,
A void exists from being a part.

Please strengthen my parts that are weak,
My heart is open, and my mind can see,
The work you are doing,
Is what's best for me.

I will continue to trust in you,
I know you will be there,
I'll keep my faith and hope alive,
You'll protect me everywhere.

In Love
~ Michael ~

1/16/12   **Someone Special**

I met someone special,
Who I like, and could possibly love,
It scares me to think this way,
So I ask God, to guide me from above.

There are days we don't speak,
She's sweet, beautiful, happy and kind,
But I know she's there,
And she's on my mind.

She's amazingly special,
An Angel in disguise,
I smile when I see her,
She's sunshine to my eyes.

Sometimes I say too much,
More than I should,
But my heart is telling me,
If I could love her… I would.

She needs her time,
And she needs her space,
I respect that greatly,
And I love her face.

I've not felt this way,
In a very long time,
I'm sensitive to her feelings,
With hope, our feelings will align.

In Love,
~ Michael ~

1/20/12 **An Open Mind**

An open mind,
Is what we need.
So we understand what's right,
And then take heed.

When our minds are open,
We receive things well,
We're less likely to harshly judge,
And not so apt, for bad things to tell.

An open mind,
With an open heart,
Will guide your spirit,
And set you apart.

With an open mind,
You'll see things more clearly,
And keep you from hurting,
The ones you love dearly.

In Love
~Michael~

7/8/12 **HE Came To Me**

HE came to me one day,
But I did not see,
But HE came back again,
Because HE, needed me.

HE comes back now,
More and more each day,
The really cool thing is,
I'm beginning, to see things His way.

So now I watch,
And listen and pray,
Because today could be, the day HE says,
You're finally doing things my way.

It's hard to know,
When HE's near to me,
Because My Eyes, My Heart, and My Ears,
Aren't always open enough, you see.

So I ask Him and say,
Please help me to see clear,
Because the better I see,
I'll see that you are near.

In Love,
~ Michael ~

7/14/12   **Forget Me Not**

Forget me not,
I never could,
Remembering you,
Is doing what I should.

The memory of you,
Is clear to me,
In my mind's eye,
You will forever be.

Your face and your smile,
Were always happy and bright,
Now that you're gone,
The Lord guides your light.

It's not about forgetting,
But remembering, that's true,
These words are written as proof,
That I'll always, remember you.

Written in memory of my very special friends;
Kevin Digiammarino and Joey DiBella

In Love,
~ Michael ~

8/3/12   **It's Never Too Late**

It's never too late,
To change your way,
Why wait til' tomorrow,
Change it today.

Your way is decided,
By where your mind goes.
Control your way,
Not like the wind blows.

It's never too late,
To do what you need,
But the time is now,
So time, is what to heed.

Some say it's too late,
Because they've given up,
Make it happen now and taste success,
It's a sweet tasting cup.

Success is not measured;
By riches alone,
If it's Sins versus Blessings,
Then it's time to atone.

In Love,
~ Michael ~

You Can't Change
The *TRUTH,*
But, The *TRUTH,*
Can Change . . .
YOUR LIFE . . .
It's *SIMPLE !*

5/11/13   **Happy Days**

Happy days come and go,
But we determine,
If they're happy you know.

Some days will be happy,
Some days will be sad,
It doesn't matter, what kind of day it is,
Be thankful, for the day you had.

We have the power to choose,
How good our day will be,
Enjoy your day and your life,
And you'll always live hap-py.

Every day should be a happy day.
No matter what happens to us.
Sometimes, we're too quick to complain.
Relax a bit, life's too short for so much fuss.

Enjoy each day,
Make it a happy one,
You think you have it tough,
Remember the acts, of God's only son.

In Love,
~ Michael ~

6/3/13   **If I Had One Wish...**

If I had one wish,
What would it be?
A wish for someone else?
Or for selfish me?

Would one wish grant me;
All the things that I seek?
Would my wish be boastful?
Or maybe, humble & meek?

If I had one wish,
With it, would I be wise?
Use it to help others?
Or for me, see how much it buys?

One wish is a gift,
What would I do?
Keep it for myself?
Or share it with you?

We all want that one wish,
But really, we want more,
Could you be satisfied, with just one?
Or can you trust, what God has in store?

In Love,
~ Michael ~

6/30/13   **The Time We Share**

The time we share,
You can't replace.
You bring a tear to my eye.
And put a smile on my face.

The time we share,
We share it now.
My time with you,
Is really, WOW!

The time we share,
It's so special to me.
I miss you when you're gone,
But my eyes light up, when it's you I see.

The time we share is cherished,
It's priceless and costly too.
The time we share together,
Makes me realize, why I love you.

In Love,
~ Michael ~

"Your Special Thoughts To Remember"...

"Your Special Thoughts To Remember"...

"Your Special Thoughts To Remember"…

"Your Special Thoughts To Remember"...

"Your Special Thoughts To Remember"...

Printed in the United States
By Bookmasters